...*We* Have This *Treasure*...

Messages to Encourage The Heart

Bobbie J Hays

WESTBOW
PRESS®
A DIVISION OF THOMAS NELSON
& ZONDERVAN

WestBow Press books may be ordered through booksellers or by contacting:

WestBow Press
A Division of Thomas Nelson & Zondervan
1663 Liberty Drive
Bloomington, IN 47403
www.westbowpress.com
844-714-3454

ISBN: 978-1-6642-0375-4 (sc)
ISBN: 978-1-6642-0376-1 (e)

Library of Congress Control Number: 2020916749

Print information available on the last page.

WestBow Press rev. date: 10/16/2020

But we have this treasure in earthen vessels, that the excellency of the power may be of God, and not of us. 2 Corinthians 4:7, KJV

That your faith should not stand in the wisdom of men, but in the power of God.
1 Corinthians 2:5, KJV

But we have this treasure in jars of clay, to show that the surpassing power belongs to God and not to us.
2 Corinthians 4:7, ESV

So that your faith might not rest in the wisdom of men but in the power of God.
1 Corinthians 2:5, ESV

If you only look at us, you might well miss the brightness. We carry this precious Message around in the unadorned clay pots of our ordinary lives. That's to prevent anyone from confusing God's incomparable power with us. 2 Corinthians 4:7, MSG

CONTENTS

Acknowledgements...ix

Preface xi

Introduction..xiii

On Eagles' Wings...1

How Shall They Preach?..5

Come See A Man 9

Why Minister? 15

The Measure of a Man 19

Footrace and Floods 25

The Wonderful Works of God................................31

Hold Your Peace...37

Time Waits for No One 41

Prayer..43

The Corinthian Song...45

About the Author 47

Acknowledgements

I thank and give praise to our Lord and Savior Jesus Christ, in whom we live, move and have our being.

I acknowledge my sons, Thado "Nick" Hays and Dr. Terrance "Nate" Hays and their spouses Terika and Turkeesha, and my adorable grandchildren: Aviance, Makayla, Kierstain, Thado Jeremiah, Mason, Kayden, Terrance,Jr., and Major for their love and support.

I acknowledge our deceased mother, Emma Griffin Skinner (March 7,1932-August 19,1991) who loved her children with an unconditional love.

I acknowledge my siblings who support my efforts and give me the space I need to complete projects.

I acknowledge my spiritual families and thank you for your prayers and support.

I acknowledge friends who support me with prayers and encouragement.

I acknowledge Men of God and Women of God who have impacted my life in numerous ways.

PREFACE

But we have this treasure in earthen vessels, that the excellency of the power may be of God, and not of us (2 Corinthians 4:7, KJV). We have been bought with a price. Because we have been purchased with the blood which Christ shed at Calvary, that makes us God's children and joint heirs with Christ. Because of this God has entrusted us to be partakers of his holiness. Although we are indeed special, we still are considered servants of the Most High. That is how we become great in the kingdom of God.

We are holy because God's spirit resides in us. When we walk in holiness, his spirit radiates on the outside. Let us keep in mind, it is not us that men see, but it is Christ in us, the hope of glory. God has chosen something fragile and unimpressive to carry his message so people would know the power is from Him and not us. We are merely the containers, vessels. The power of the gospel is not limited by the quality of its containers. We are limited, but God's gospel is not.

We have this treasure. We carry the powerful word of God on the inside. When we open our mouths and speak it, it has a positive effect on those who hear it. I know this because the Word of God does not return to him void, but it accomplishes in the thing whereto he sends it (Isaiah 55:11, KJV).

This word is hidden in our hearts that we may not sin against God (Psalm 119:11, KJV). Even when we do sin, we have an advocate with the Father, Jesus Christ the righteous. (1 John 2:1b, KJV) If we confess our sins, God is faithful and just to forgive us our sins and to cleanse us from all unrighteousness (1 John 1:9, KJV).

The word of God is a treasure on the inside of us. Therefore when we speak kind words or do good deeds, it's not us. It is the power of God working through us. We are vessels full of God's power. We are earthen vessels, clay that God used to form man in his image (Genesis 1:27, KJV).

Although we have this treasure, we are troubled on every side, yet not distressed; we are perplexed, but not in despair; persecuted, but not forsaken; cast down, but not destroyed; always bearing about in the body the dying of the Lord Jesus, that the life also of Jesus might be made manifest in our mortal flesh (2 Corinthians 4:4-11, KJV). Our suffering is enormous, but we will not be wiped out. But even if we are, we will live with Christ in eternity.

Because we have this treasure, we can declare in faith, I can do all things through Christ who strengthens me (Philippians 4:19, KJV). Because we have this treasure, we can declare in faith, I am not ashamed of the gospel of Christ: for it is the power of God unto salvation to every one that believeth; to the Jew first, and also to the Greek (Romans 1:16, KJV). The gospel of Christ is not limited by race, creed, or color. It knows no bounds. Because we have this treasure, we do not fear, because we know that there is no fear in love, but perfect love casteth out fear; because fear hath torment. He that feareth is not made perfect in love (1 John 4:18 KJV).

Finally, we have this treasure because He giveth power to the faint; and to them that have no might he increaseth strength. Even the youth shall faint and be weary, and the young men shall utterly fall; But they that wait upon the Lord shall renew their strength; they shall mount up with wings as eagles; they shall run, and not be weary, and they shall walk and not faint (Isaiah 40:29-31, KJV).

INTRODUCTION

In the words of H. Beecher Hicks, Jr., from his book My
Soul's Been Anchored, "God's work is larger than we
are. God has a way, however, of using us in spite of us."
"Even more," he goes on to say, "everyone God called
was not qualified for the job. Noah was a drunk.

Abraham was a liar.
Moses was a murderer.
David was a philanderer.
Jeremiah was a crybaby.
Sampson was a ladies' man.
Matthew was an extortioner.
Thomas was a doubter.
Peter was a man who denied his Lord."

Every preacher God called never quite deserved the title. But God
calls undeserving preachers and uses us, despite what we are. God
looks beyond who we are to who we can become.

Though I too have long since entered the second half-century
of my life, I realize I have not lived up to models in whose midst I
have had the opportunity to sit. None of us have become who God
would have us become as ministers of the gospel or as individuals,
for we are yet under construction.

In this anthology, it is my prayerful aim to share with the
readers some messages that will hopefully encourage hearts, uplift
spirits, and lead still others to make a decision to trust in the
saving grace of our Lord and Savior Jesus Christ.

ON EAGLES' WINGS

Exodus 19:4–6 (KJV)

Ye have seen what I did unto the Egyptians, and how I bore you on eagles' wings, and brought you unto myself. Now therefore, if ye will obey my voice indeed, and keep my covenant, then ye shall be a peculiar treasure unto me above all people: for all the earth is mine.

And ye shall be unto me a kingdom of priests, and an holy nation. These are the words which thou shalt speak unto the children of Israel. (Exodus 19:4–6 KJV)

God took time to remind the Israelites of three vital truths. We, too, must be reminded of these truths. First of all, God reminds them of the love He had for them. Secondly, He reminds them of the victories He had won for them. And thirdly, He reminds them of the future He planned for them. God had a great love for the Israelites. So much love that He had his servant Moses remind them, "Ye have seen what I did unto the Egyptians" (Exodus 19:4 KJV). God sent ten disasters on Egypt in order to force the Pharaoh to allow the children of Israel to depart from slavery. These plagues served as signs and marvels to let Pharaoh

1

know that he does not know God. This would cause them to know that the Lord is God. He goes on to say, "And how I bore you (the Israelites) on eagles' wings, and brought you unto myself" (Exodus 19:4 KJV).

> As an eagle stirreth up her nest, fluttereth over her young, spreadeth abroad her wings, taketh them, beareth them on her wings. (Deuteronomy 32:11 KJV)

> God was like an eagle hovering over its nest, overshadowing its young. Then spreading its wings, lifting them into the air, teaching them to fly. (Deuteronomy 32:11 MSG)

Sometimes God has to shake us up. We sometimes get too complacent in our comfort zones. He stirs us up. He causes us to take off the training wheels of our lives. He wants us to take those words He has spoken to us and apply them to our lives. We have a tendency to get so weighed down with the cares of this life that we forget to cast our cares upon Him. God won many victories for the Israelites. Like the Israelites, how soon we forget when God has won a victory for us. Psalm 136 makes mention of some of the victories God won for them. Each victory in scripture here is followed by the phrase "For his mercy endureth forever." I take this to mean that He will do it again and again if He has to. Some of these victories include:

> ... smote Egypt in their firstborn.
> ... For his mercy endures forever
> ... brought out Israel from among them.
> ... For his mercy endures forever
> ... divided the Red Sea into parts.
> ... For his mercy endures forever
> ... made Israel to past through the midst of it.

… For his mercy endures forever
… overthrew Pharaoh and his host in the Red Sea.
… For his mercy endures forever
… led his people through the wilderness.
… For his mercy endures forever
… smote great kings.
… For his mercy endures forever
… Sihon king of the Amorites.
… For his mercy endures forever
… and Og the king of Bashan.
… For his mercy endures forever
… gave their land for an heritage.
… For his mercy endures forever
… remembered us in our low estate.
… For his mercy endures forever
… hath redeemed us from or enemies.
… For his mercy endures forever
… who giveth food to all flesh. (Psalm 139:10–25)
… For his mercy endures forever

The future He'd planned for them. Jeremiah 29:11 (KJV) declares these words of the Lord: "For I know the thoughts that I think toward you, saith the Lord, thoughts of peace, and not of evil, to give you an expected end." That same passage in the Message Bible says this, "I know what I am doing. I have it all planned out—plans to take care of you, not abandon you, plans to give you the future you hope for." If the Israelites would obey God's voice and keep his covenant, they would be a peculiar treasure unto Him above all people. They would be to God a kingdom of priests and a holy nation (Exodus 19:5 KJV).

God has a great plan for each of His children. One way he executes that plan when He sent His only son to die for us on a cross at Calvary, allowed Him to be buried, and raised Him from the grave on the third day with all the power of heaven and earth in His hands. "For whosoever believes in their heart and confesses with their mouth this truth can enjoy the blessedness of eternal life" (Romans 10:9 KJV).

God has not ceased to win victories. He challenges us as He did the Israelites in Exodus 14:14 (KJV), which says, "The Lord shall fight for you, and ye shall hold your peace."

God does not want us to be afraid. He says, "Fear ye not, stand still, and see the salvation of the Lord" (Exodus 14:13b KJV).

Many times we doubt God because we can't see around the corner, but God can. This is why we have to learn to trust him. Do what he says. He's not going to lead us wrong. He loves us too much for that. Remember the love God has for you. Even while we were dead in our trespasses and sins, Christ died for us (Romans 5:8 KJV).

Remember the victories the Lord has won for you, the prayers He has answered for you, the diseases He has healed for you, the protection He has given you, all the provisions He has made for you, the enemies He has defeated for you, the darkness He has kept back from your life, and all the dangers from which He has kept you.

Remember all the times the Lord has restored your soul and caused you to lie down in green pastures (Psalm 23:2, 3 KJV).

He is the same God now that He was then. Therefore, I challenge us all to "be careful for nothing; but in every thing by prayer and supplication with thanksgiving let your requests be made known unto God, and the peace of God which passeth all understanding, shall keep your hearts and minds through Christ Jesus" (Philippians 4:6, 7 KJV).

How Shall They Preach?

> And how shall they preach, except they be sent? As
> it is written, How beautiful are the feet of them that
> preach the gospel of peace and bring glad tidings of
> good things! (Romans 10:15)

The apostle Paul in chapter 10 of Romans knew that in order for
one to preach God's Word effectively one must be sent by the
Holy Spirit. We, too, must realize that in order to do anything
worthwhile for God, we must be sent or assigned to do it. When
God sends you, your way has already been made.

I believe there are at least three things we can draw from this
passage as it relates to a preacher of the gospel. One thing for
certain is that as a minister of the gospel, we must declare like the
apostle Paul the following: "For I am not ashamed of the gospel
of Christ, for it is the power of God unto salvation to every one
that believeth; to the Jew first, and also to the Greek" (Romans
1:16 KJV). Paul wasn't ashamed because this gospel belonged to
Christ. The power of it belonged to God, and the purpose of it was
to save the soul of everyone who believed in it. If you go against
the grain, you get splinters, regardless of which neighborhood
you're from, what your parents taught you, or what schools you
attended. But if you embrace the way God does things, there are
wonderful payoffs—which, again, are given without regard to

where you are from or how you were brought up (Romans 2:9, 10 MSG).

Another thing we must realize is that one must be sent. In order for one to carry the gospel of Jesus Christ, he or she must be sent. In other words, told to go (consider Isaiah 6:8-10, KJV).

Luke 10:3 (KJV) tells us, "Go your ways: behold, I send you forth as lambs among wolves." The word "wolves" refers to danger. As you preach the gospel, sometimes you will face real danger. Jesus knows how violently people can respond when their religious pride and hypocrisy are exposed. The world can be hostile to those who carry the gospel, but danger gives the disciples no excuse to withdraw from the assignment.

Like Jesus Himself they are not to prepare to defend themselves or to minister in their own strength. They are to depend solely on God, taking with them no provisions—no moneybags, knapsacks, or extra pairs of sandals. They were to allow God to provide for them. In addition, a preacher must wear the right shoes to do the job assigned. His or her feet must be shod with readiness to spread the gospel of peace (Ephesians 6:16 KJV).

Readiness involves preparation. Preparation involves prayer and study. It involves sometimes even reading other works. In other words, refuse to stand before God's people empty.

The scripture teaches us that the feet are beautiful—the feet are beautiful because they trod in places where the good news need to be shared. No matter what the conditions or circumstances, the preacher has to be able to stand for what is right, for what is loving, for what is just, and for what is oftentimes against the status quo.

The Roman soldier wore hobnailed sandals with cleat-like studs underneath so that no matter how slippery the ground, he could stand firm-footed in hand-to-hand combat. We can stand unmoved against the foe when our feet are firmly planted on the solid rock. This rock is Jesus! He's the one. Our Lord in His ministry went against the grain. He saw a need and met it and didn't care who didn't like it. He healed on the sabbath, though it was against Pharisaic laws (Mark 3:5 KJV).

His disciples plucked corn and ate it on the sabbath, although that was considered as work (Mark 2:23, 24 KJV).

Wearing the correct shoes involves standing on the promises of Christ the Savior, knowing that the One who has called you will equip you and provide for you.

Finally, the preacher must share the good news. This news is of the saving grace of Jesus Christ. The news that, For God so loved the world that he gave his only begotten Son that whosoever believeth in him shall not perish, but shall have everlasting life. (John 3:16, KJV)

The good news that all have sinned and come short of the glory of God, but God commended his love toward us in that while we were yet sinners Christ died for us. (Romans 3:23, 5:8, KJV)

The news that if thou shalt confess with thy mouth the Lord Jesus, and believe in thine heart that God hath raised him from the dead, thou shalt be saved. (Romans 10:9) The news that Jesus suffered, bled and died. O yes, he died. He was buried in a borrowed tomb. But the good news is he didn't stay there. On the third-day morning he got up and later declared, All power is given unto me in heaven and in earth. (Matthew 28:18, KJV) The news that He went away, but He's coming back. (Acts 1:11, KJV) How shall they preach? The preacher must be sent; the preacher must wear the right footing; the preacher must share the good news of the gospel.

COME SEE A MAN

John 4:1-14; 28, 29, KJV

The Writer: John the Baptist, a forerunner of Jesus Christ, is the one who shouted, This is the one who said, He it is, who coming after me is preferred before me, whose shoe's latchet I am not worthy to unloose. (John 1:27 KJV) John is the one who said, Behold the Lamb of God, which taketh away the sin of the world. (John 1:29, KJV) What a task it must have been to have to introduce Jesus!

I can imagine having to introduce Jesus. I would probably say, Jesus is the wind beneath my wings, the Treasure I seek, the foundation on which I build, the Song in my heart, the Object of my desire; the Breath of my life, He is my all in All; He is Alpha and Omega; He is the Beginning and the End; He is the Ancient of Days; the Anointed One, the Chief Cornerstone, the Dayspring, The Door, the Everlasting Father, Firstborn over all creation, the Great Head of the Church. He is the Way, the Truth and the Life. In John's gospel we learn a lot about who Jesus is by observing what He said and did when he was with other people. These include a Samaritan woman who received Jesus' offer of life-giving water, a woman who had been caught in sin; (John 4, KJV), his friend Lazarus who was brought back to life by Jesus, (John 11, KJV) and his follower Thomas who doubted that

Jesus was raised from the dead.(John 20:25, KJV) In this book Jesus performs seven miracles. Each of them is a sign that tells us something about Jesus as the Son of God. By healing a lame man, (John 5, KJV), Jesus shows that he is just like his Father who never stops working. My Father works hitherto and I work.(John 5:17, KJV); I must work the works of Him that sent me while it is day: the night cometh, when no man can work. (John 9:4, KJV).

In John's gospel we find Jesus engaged in long conversations with people about who he is and what he has come to do. In these conversations he teaches that he is the way, the truth, and the life. No man comes to the Father but by me. (John 14:6, KJV). In this text Jesus left Judea and started for Galilee. This time he had a need to go through Samaria, and on his way he came to the town Sychar. It was near a field that Jacob had long ago given to his son Joseph. The well that Jacob had dug was still there, and Jesus sat down beside it because he was tired from traveling. It is alright to sit down and rest when you're tired from doing the Lord's work. This Samaritan woman was tired of the lifestyle she was living and didn't know it. She was coming to draw water at a time when none of the other women would be there because she knew they would be talking about her and to keep from dealing with this she just came at a time when no one else would be there. Genesis 24:11, KJV, informs us that women drew water in the late evening when it was cool and the sun had gone down, not in the heat of the day. The Bible says it was noon when this woman came (John 4:6, KJV). One thing we can surmise from this:

Jesus meets us where we are. Since the Samaritan woman had come to draw water and that seem to be the business of the hour, he asked her, would you give me a drink? This woman is no stranger to thirst. After all, she is at the well to draw water. She has been divorced five times and is living with a boyfriend when she meets Jesus. Here is a woman who is thirsty for a lasting, durable and stable relationship. Here is a woman thirsting for meaning and direction in her life. I believe the deepest need of every person is God. Whether he admits it or not, man is thirsty for God. Psalm 42:1, 2, KJV declares, As the hart panteth after the water brooks, so panteth my soul after thee, O God. My soul thirsteth for God, for the living God: when shall I come and appear before God? How is it that thou, being a Jew, askest drink of me, which am a woman of Samaria? (John 4:9b, KJV) The woman had to think Jesus didn't know that. If you are having problems in areas of finance, He is going to meet you there and suggest to you to sow seeds in that area or possibly tithe; if you are having problems with a boyfriend or girlfriend, He just might ask you to spend more time with Him; It could be in prayer or it could just be his wanting to spend time alone with you. If you are having problems on your job, and you are trying to fix everything that's broken,

He is trying to tell you, turn it all over to me and allow me to fix it for you. He will probably ask you, Come unto me all who labor and I will give you rest…? With this woman the problem wasn't physical water, but that was a good starting point because she would meet someone who could give her the water of life that would well up inside her when she was thirsty or lonely or just needed someone with whom to talk. She wouldn't have to pick up the phone every time she needed to know something or turn on the T.V. set, but the Holy Spirit would teach her and bring to her remembrance the things he had taught her. Not only does Jesus meet us where we are, but He is the only one who knows our business and won't discuss it with anyone but you. Jesus had so dealt with this woman that she was now asking him to give her that living water so that she wouldn't have to come to the well again. (John 4:15, KJV, paraphrased) This is right where he wanted her. Now he can really deal with her. He says to her in verse 16 of John 4, Go, call thy husband, and come hither. Jesus is now addressing the thing that is causing her not to be able to come to draw water with the other women. He is addressing this issue so that she can be free. And we know whom the Lord makes free is free indeed. Go and bring your husband.

Whatever it is that is causing you trouble, go and bring it to Jesus.

The woman answered and said, I have no husband. She hits the nail on the head. Jesus said unto her, thou has well said, I have no husband: For thou hast had five husbands; and he whom thou now hast is not thy husband: in that sadist thou truly. (John 4: 17, 18 KJV)

By the time she left Jesus, she had forgotten her initial visit to the well. But this woman was so full of living water, that she left her water pot and began to advertise for Jesus. Come see a man, which told me all things that ever I did: is not this the Christ? (John 4:29, KJV)

Not only does Jesus meet us where we are; not only does he know everything about us, but He changes our direction. Instead of the woman going back to that dead end situation she was in, she went back to town and told the people to come see a man. She began to evangelize and advertise for Jesus. (John 4:29, KJV).

Everyone in the town went out to see Jesus. (John 4:30, KJV) How do you advertise for Christ? First of all, put no confidence in the flesh. What you got on and how much it cost or didn't cost. Whether the nails are long enough or have the right kind of polish. How much weave your neighbor has or whether or not it is a weave. These things are fleshly-put no confidence in them- your talent, your job, your education, who you know or don't know. You have got to know that you are looking good from the inside out. If you have not spent any time with the Lord across the week in prayer, in meditation and reading your Bible, doing something good for someone other than yourself- it will show up.

How do you advertise for Christ? Next, take your eyes off everybody else and keep your eyes on Jesus. You are worth just as much without stuff as you are with stuff. Of course man looks on the outward appearance, but God looks on the heart. (1 Samuel 16:7, KJV) For I say, through the grace given unto me, to every man that is among you, not to think of himself more highly than he ought to think; but to think soberly, according as God hath dealt to every man the measure of faith. (Romans 12:3, KJV).

How do you advertise for Christ? Be humble in the presence of God's mighty power; and he will honor you when the time comes. Don't depend on things like fancy hairdos or gold jewelry or expensive clothes to make you look beautiful. Be beautiful in your heart by being gentle and of a quiet spirit. This kind of beauty will last.

I invite you to Come see a man-a man who is able to turn your midnights into days- a Man who will meet you where you are- a Man who will keep in confidence whatever you share with Him and a Man who can and will change your direction. This Man is Jesus Christ, the Son of the living God.

WHY MINISTER?

Knowing therefore the terror of the Lord, we persuade men; but we are made manifest unto God; and I trust also are made manifest in your consciences. For we commend not ourselves again unto you, but give you occasion to glory on our behalf that ye may have somewhat to answer them which glory in appearance, and not in heart. (2 Corinthians 5:11, 12, KJV)

What we believe and how we behave must always go together. When this does not happen, it usually means that our heart is divided. Because of what God has done for us should motivate us to do something for God. So then what is the ministry of the children of God? To persuade or convince sinners to be reconciled to God. We don't force people to trust Christ, nor do we use devious means. We persuade men through this glorious Gospel of our Lord and Savior Jesus Christ. The Apostle Paul said, I am not ashamed of the gospel of Christ; for it is the power of God unto salvation; to everyone who believeth, to the Jew first and also to the Greek (Romans 1:16, KJV).

The child of God must have the right motive for ministry as well as the right message.

For some strange reason the younger generation does not seem to be taking the things of God seriously. Could it be that we are not reverencing God or His Holy Word? Could it be that we talk too casually about God as if He's just one of the guys? Where is the reverential fear our forefathers had for God? The Judaizers ministered to please men but Paul ministered to please Jesus alone.

In Galatians 1:10, KJV, he says, For do I now persuade men or God? Or do I seek to please men? For if I yet pleased men, I should not be the servant of Christ. A man pleasing ministry is carnal and it's compromising. God cannot bless it. Not only should we persuade men but we must do what we do with a clear conscience. Paul was not afraid of what his enemies were saying because he knew that his conscience was clear. Paul tells them I gave you my testimony. I know what I use to do, but God called me by His grace and but by the grace of God I am what I am today. Yes he persecuted the church of God but he has a testimony of how the Lord blinded him and saved him and delivered him and put him in the ministry. The truth about each one of us shall be revealed and Jesus Christ will commend us for the things that have pleased Him.

Thirdly, we must be careful not to depend on the praise of men. In 2 Corinthians 5:12, KJV, we find, For we commend not ourselves again unto you, but give you occasion to glory on our behalf, that ye may have somewhat to answer them which glory in appearance, and not in heart. The Message Bible says of that passage, "We're not saying this to make ourselves look good to you. We just thought it would make you feel good, proud even, that we're on your side and not just nice to your face as so many people are." We must realize we are on the same team. There is no need for us to strive with or fight against one another. Let us encourage one another in the faith. The Judaizers in Paul's day took great pride in "letters of commendation." For example, we are sometimes heard to say I want to thank Sister Jones for that fine prayer. First of all, the prayer wasn't to you; it was to God. So let God thank Sister Jones.

If we live only for the praise of men, we will not win the praise of God. When we live only for man's praise we are exalting reputation over character. It's our character that's going to count when we see Christ. The only valid commendation for effective ministry is changed lives.

Our motive for ministry to win people to Christ is our own convictions. It compels us to want to share the good news of the saving grace of Christ. He is not just an ordinary person. He's not just a good man. He's not just a charismatic teacher. He is the greatest person who ever walked the face of this earth.

Another reason why we want to win people to Christ is because we are convinced that Jesus changes people's lives. Therefore if any man be in Christ, he is a new creature; old things are passed away, behold all things are become new (2 Corinthians 5:17, KJV).

Another motive for ministry is that God gave us this ministry. We are suppose to be doing what we're doing. God has given us the ministry of reconciliation (2 Corinthians 5:18b, KJV). The ministry of reconciliation is that God was reconciling the world to himself in Christ, not counting men's sins against them. And he has committed to us the message of reconciliation. God has given us the responsibility of sharing this message any way we can. Whether it is through feeding the homeless, clothing the naked, praying for the sick, or on a mission field in some other country. As believers in Christ our job is to help people be restored in their relationship with God. God has saved me by his grace.

Because we are saved does not mean life is going to be a bed of roses. We can have the abundant life, but just know it comes with some suffering. If you suffer with Him, you will also reign with Him. (2 Timothy 2:12, KJV) It comes with afflictions, but the Lord delivers us out of them all. (Psalm 34:19, KJV) It comes with adversities, but remember we are more than conquers through Him that loved us. (Romans 3:37, KJV)

THE MEASURE OF A MAN

And he said unto them, Take heed, and beware of covetousness; for a man's life consisteth not in the abundance of the things which he possesseth. -Luke 12:15, KJV

Temperature is measured by degrees.

Weight is measured in pounds.

Speed is measured by miles per hour.

Liquid is measured in ounces.

Distance is measured by miles.

Time is measured in seconds, minutes, hours.

Hard drives are measured by megabytes.

Pressure is measured by PSI.

Genius is measured by IQ.

True manhood is measured by Virtues.

Gillis Triplett, Mastering Manhood

The true measure of a man is his merciful and gracious dealing with other people. Till we all come in the unity of the faith, and of the knowledge of the Son of God, unto a perfect man, unto the measure of the stature of the fullness of Christ (Ephesians 4:13, KJV). Unto a perfect man means until we all become full grown in the Lord.

Have you ever seen people who always look down on other people because they might not have what they have? If we are guilty of this, we need to stop it right this instance. None of us can afford to look down at someone else because they might not drive a nice car or live in a big house, or wear the finest of raiment. Jesus taught that the world seen from God's viewpoint is tilted in favor of those who might not have it all so to speak. At this point, a man in the crowd interrupted Jesus and asked Him to solve a family problem. Rabbis were expected to help settle legal matters, but Jesus refused to get involved. Because he knew that no answer He gave would solve the real problem, which was covetousness in the hearts of the two brothers. As long as both men were greedy, no settlement would be satisfactory. Their greatest need was to have their hearts changed. Like too many people today, they want Jesus to serve them but not to save them.

Solomon was one of the wealthiest men in the world and the Lord said that Solomon in all his glory was not arrayed like the lilies of the field. (Matthew 6:29, KJV)

Job had many riches, but one day it was all taken away. Yet God referred to him as a perfect and an upright man who feared God and eschewed evil. (Job 1: 8, KJV) But Jesus says you can not measure a man by what he has. And he said unto them, Take heed, and beware of covetousness; for a man's life consisteth not in the abundance of the things which he possesseth. (Luke 12:15, KJV) The Message Bible says it this way, Speaking to the people, he went on, "take care! Protect yourself against the least bit of greed. Life is not defined by what you have, even when you have a lot. (Luke 12:15, MSG)

So then, who are you without your stuff?

Covetousness is an unquenchable thirst for getting more and more of something we think we need in order to be truly satisfied. It may be a thirst for money or the things that money can buy, or even a thirst for position and power. Jesus made it clear that true life does not depend on an abundance of possessions.

How do you measure? Well, one way is lessons from opposites. When our Lord entered our world He modeled a different perspective on things. In coming and dying for our sins, he in essence said, The way up is down ... the way to find happiness is to become a servant and put the needs of others first.

And this is exactly opposite of the way our society tends to look at things. The vast majority of the people in our country tend to think that the way up is up ... the way to gain is to get. They tend to think that to do otherwise would be absurd. Bill Hybels writes In the Vocabulary of our World, Down is a word reserved for losers and cowards. It is a word to be avoided and ignored ... it is a word that negatively colors whatever it touches. We say: down and out, downfall, downscale, downhearted and worst of all, down under. And down's antonym is Up ... a word in our high voltage society that has come to be cherished and worshiped..a word reserved to describe winners and heroes. Unlike the word down, "up" positively colors whatever it touches. We say things like: Upscale, Up and coming, Upper class, and Upwardly mobile. We believe in ascending to fame, money, power, comfort, and pleasure. In our society Up is clearly the direction to greatness. From the world's perspective, it is the only way to go.

But you know like a tidal wave, Jesus crashed into our worldly way of thinking and flips things. He turns everything upside down by teaching that if you truly want to be great, you must go down. You must descend into greatness. Then arose a reasoning among them, which of them should be greatest. And Jesus, perceiving the thought of their heart, took a child, and set him by him, and said unto them, whosoever shall receive this child in my name receiveth me and whosoever shall receiveth him that sent me; for he that is least among you all, the same shall be great. (Luke 9:46,

KJV). Our care for others is a measure of our greatness. How much care to you show to others? This is what I believe measures our greatness in God's eyes.

And he sat down, and called the twelve, and saith unto them, If any man desire to be first, the same shall be last of all, and servant of all. (Mark 9:35, KJV)

But many that are first shall be last; and the last shall be first. (Matthew 19:30, KJV)

But many that are first shall be last; and the last first. (Mark 10:31, KJV)

And, behold, there are last which shall be first, and there are first which shall be last. (Luke 13:30, KJV)

In the lesson from opposites we find that the way up is down.

For whosoever exalteth himself shall be abased; and he that humbleth himself shall be exalted.

(Luke 14:11, KJV)

I tell you, this man went down to his house justified rather than the other; for every one that exalteth himself shall be abased; and he that humbleth himself shall be exalted. (Luke 18:14, KJV)

With the world you get by getting; with Jesus you get by giving. Give and it shall be given unto you, good measure, pressed down, shaken together, and running over, shall men give into your bosom. For with the same measure you mete withal it shall be measured to you again. (Luke 6:38, KJV) We get by giving.

Life does not consist of abundant possessions. Greed is an insatiable desire for more; more money, more gold, more silver, more possessions, more toys, more land, more cattle. The greedy person is never satisfied. There never comes a moment when he or she says "enough." It reminds me of a passage in Proverbs 30:15b-16, KJV: There are three things that are never satisfied, yea, four things say not, It is enough: the grave; and the barren womb; the earth that is not filled with water; and the fire that saith not, It is enough.

This means that the man who petitioned Jesus in Luke 12:13, KJV, will not have his problem resolved if Jesus intervenes on his behalf and if his brother gives him what he wants. He might be satisfied for a while but he won't be satisfied for long. There will come a time when greed will raise its ugly head again. So Jesus says, Take heed, and beware of covetousness; for a man's life consisteth not in the abundance of the things which he possesseth. (Luke12:15, KJV) He is judged most successful who has the most money, the most expensive car, the biggest investment portfolio, the most recreational vehicles and the biggest home. Jesus is not saying it is wrong to have riches. Nor is he saying it is wrong to have a saving plan or an IRA. What Jesus is saying is that a greater abundance of goods does not mean a greater abundance of life.

Jesus drives home this point by telling the man and the crowd the Parable of the Rich Fool. (Luke 12:16-21, KJV). In this parable we see a man who is already rich. On top of this, with no extra effort on his part, he is given even more riches through God's gift of a bumper crop. He did not earn it and he did not need it.

This unearned and unneeded wealth gives the rich man a problem: what to do with his unexpected windfall. Anybody ever had an unexpected windfall?

The rich man has something in mind that he's going to do with this increase. He is storing his unexpected wealth, keeping it safe, for his future well-being. He is planning to take life easy; he does not have to do any more work; he can surround himself with servants to do his every bidding and doesn't have to lift a finger. With all his wealth he can now eat, drink, and be merry without a care in the world.

God, however, has something entirely different in mind. But God said unto him, Thou fool, this night thy soul shall be required of thee; then whose shall these things be, which thou hast provided? Let us ponder and consider these scriptures:

But godliness with contentment is great gain. (1 Timothy 6:6, KJV) We should honor God and center our lives on him and we should be content with what God is doing in our lives.

As we have therefore opportunity, let us do good unto all men, especially unto them who are of the household of faith. (Galatians 6:10, KJV) Keep on doing what is right and trust God for the results. In due time, we will reap a harvest of blessing.

Lay not up for yourselves treasures upon earth, where moth and rust doth corrupt, and where thieves break through and steal; But lay up for yourselves treasures in heaven, where neither moth nor rust doth corrupt, and where thieves do not break through and steal; For where your treasure is, there will your heart be also. (Matthew 6:19-21, KJV) Use all you have for the glory of God. Hang loose when it comes to the material things of life.

Not that I speak in respect of want; for I have learned, in whatsoever state I am, therewith to be content. (Philippians 4:11, KJV). If you always want more, ask God to remove that desire and teach you contentment in every situation. He will supply all your needs, but in a way that he knows is best for you.

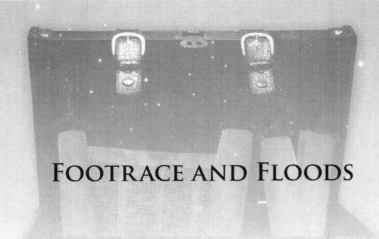

FOOTRACE AND FLOODS

> If thou hast run with the footmen, and they have
> wearied thee, then how canst thou contend with
> horses? And if the land of peace, wherein thou
> trustedst, they wearied thee, then how wilt thou do
> in the swelling of the Jordan?
>
> Jeremiah 12:5, KJV

The Man

When you think of success, what do you think about? Do you
think of successful people as those who enjoy the good-life-
financially and emotionally secure, with lots of admirers and
enjoying the fruits of their labors?

Most successful people are leaders, opinion makers and
trendsetters. They usually know who they are or where they're
going and they strive to meet their goals.

By these standards Jeremiah was a miserable failure. For forty
years he served as God's spokeman to Judah; but when Jeremiah
spoke, nobody listened.

He urged the people to act and nobody moved. He had no
material success. He was poor and underwent severe deprivation
to deliver what God told him to deliver. He was thrown into

prison-thrown in a well, rejected by his neighbors and his family. In the eyes of the world Jeremiah was not a success.

However, in God's eyes, Jeremiah was one of the most successful people in history. Success, as measured by God involves obedience and faithfulness. God told Joshua, This book of the law shall not depart out of thy mouth; but thou shalt meditate therein day and night, that thou mayest observe to do according to all that is written therein: for then thou shalt make thy way prosperous, and then thou shalt have good success. (Joshua 1:8, KJV)

Regardless of the opposition and personal cost, Jeremiah courageously and faithfully proclaimed God's word. What God asks us to do, He graces us for it; what he graces us for, He asks us to do.

The Book

You know you're reading Jeremiah (KJV) when you come across these passages:

Then I went down to the potter's house, and behold, he wrought a work on the wheels (18:3).

For I know the thoughts I have toward you saith the Lord, thoughts of peace and not of evil, to give you an expected end (29:11).

> Call unto me, and I will answer thee, and shew thee great and mighty things, which thou knowest not (33:3).

> ... but his word was in mine heart as a burning fire shut up in my bones (20:9b).

> The heart is deceitful above all things, and desperately wicked: who can know it? (17:9).

Blessed is the man who trusteth in the Lord, and whose hope the Lord is (17:7).

Thy words were found, and I did eat them; thy word was unto me the joy and rejoicing of mine heart; for I am called by thy name, O Lord God of host (15:16).

Then said the Lord unto me, Pray not for this people for their good (14:11).

The Message

If thou has run with the footmen, and they have wearied thee, then how canst thou contend with horses? And if in the land of peace, wherein thou trustedst, they wearied thee, then how wilt thou do in the swelling of Jordan? (Jeremiah 12:5, KJV)

The Amplified Bible says it like this: "If you have raced with men on foot and they have tired you out, then how can you compete with horses? If you fall down in a land of peace {where you feel secure}, then how will you do among the lions in the {flooded} thicket beside the Jordan?

It is easy to be tranquil when danger is not pressing us. The man who was wearied in a foot-race should not venture to measure his speed against that of horses.

God is able to cause us to stand firmly and progress on the dangerous heights of testing and trouble. He can make your feet like hinds feet. He did for David. (Psalm 18:33, KJV) David also said, I have run through a troop and leaped over a wall. (Psalm 18:29, KJV) He also fought a lion and a bear and won; not to mention downed Golaih. (1 Samuel 17:49, KJV)

The things the devil means for evil in your life, God can turn it around and cause it to work for your good. We can't blame the devil for doing his job. This is why He comes, to make our lives miserable. Many of us have only been dealing with minor issues. We've been running with footmen. How are you going to handle it when the really tough stuff come your way?

If Jeremiah was so soon tired in a land of peace, where there was little noise or peril, what would he do in the swelling of Jordan, when it overflows all its banks?

We have got to learn to be able to contend with horses. How do we do this?

First, we must learn how to run this race with patient expectation. Wherefore seeing we also are compassed about with so great a cloud of witnesses, let us lay aside every weight, and the sin which doth so easily beset us, and let us run with patience the race that is set before us (Hebrews 12:1, KJV). How do we contend with horses? Looking to Jesus the author and finisher of our faith. (Hebrews 12:2b, KJV)

While we are in this world we can expect troubles and difficulties. Man that is born of a woman is of a few days and that full of trouble. (Job 14:1, KJV) Look at the last question in the passage. How wilt thou do in the swelling of Jordan? Many take this to mean How do we plan to conduct ourselves in the hour of death. Also it is a personal question. The word "thou" is translated "you." It individualizes us and makes us each come face to face with a dying hour. We are too quick to regard all men as mortal, but ourselves. We can see frailty of life in other people, but not ourselves. We are blind to our own weakness. This is also a rebuke question for Jeremiah. God had already told him in Jeremiah 1:8 Be not afraid of their faces; for I am with thee to deliver thee, saith the Lord. Sometimes, however, we must counsel ourselves. Remind yourself that God is with you. Remember that God is in you and greater is he that is in you than he that is in the world. (1 John 4:4b, KJV) Recall who you are as in Jeremiah 1:18, 19, KJV, For, behold, I have made thee this day a defenced city, and an iron pillar, and a brazen wall against the whole land, against the kings of Judah, against the princes thereof, against the priests thereof, and against the people of the land. And they shall fight against thee; but they shall not prevail against thee; for I am with thee, saith the Lord, to deliver thee. The problem we face might be as overwhelming as Jeremiah's. Just know that you will not be defeated. If God be for us who can be against us? (Romans 8:31, KJV)

Jeremiah had begun to complain. Sometimes the prophet whose business is to admonish others, finds himself complaining. Part of Jeremiah's complaint was that these wicked people of Anathoth were prospering. They wearied him because it was in a land of peace wherein he trusted. It was very grievous to him to be hated and abused by his own kindred. Jeremiah was disturbed in his mind by this; his spirit was sunk and overwhelmed, so much so, that it caused great agitation and distress. He was discouraged in his work by this and began to be weary of prophesying and to think of giving up. He did not consider that this was but the beginning of his sorrow and that he had far greater trials yet before him. The book of James tells us, My brethren, count it all joy when you fall into divers temptation, knowing this that the trying of your faith worketh patience. (James 1:2, 3, KJV) No matter what trials we go through, God is working something good out in us. No trial we go through is ever wasted. It is a growth process. Be not weary in well doing for in due season you shall reap if you faint not. (Galatians 6:9, KJV)

The Wonderful Works of God

Acts 2:1-4, 11, KJV

And when the day of Pentecost was fully come, they were all with one accord in one place. And suddenly there came a sound from heaven as of a rushing mighty wind, and it filled all the house where they were sitting.

And there appeared unto them cloven tongues like as of fire, and it sat upon each of them. And they were all filled with the Holy Ghost, and began to speak with other tongues, as the Spirit gave them utterance. Cretes and Arabians, we do hear them speak in our tongues the wonderful works of God. (Acts 2:1-4, 11, KJV)

The day of Pentecost came fifty days after what we know as Easter. This would be the day that God would pour out his Spirit and empower these men and women who were assembled waiting for what the Lord had promised would come. This marked the empowerment of the church. Many thought that these believers were drunk, but the Apostle Peter assured them that this was that which was spoken by the prophet Joel; And it shall come to pass in the Last Days, saith God, I will pour out of my Spirit upon all flesh: and your sons and your daughters shall prophesy and your old men shall dream dreams: and on my servants and on my handmaidens I will pour out in those days of my Spirit, and they shall prophesy: and I will shew wonders in heaven above, and signs in the earth beneath: blood, and fire, and vapour of smoke. (Acts 2:15-19, KJV)

What then are these wonderful works of God? About 3,000 souls were added following Peter's sermon. (Acts 2:14-41, KJV) Fear came upon every soul: and many wonders and signs were done by the apostles. And all that believed were together, and had all things common. (Acts 2:43-44, KJV) And they continuing daily with one accord in the temple, and breaking bread from house to house, did eat their meat with gladness and singleness of heart. Praising God, and having favor with all the people. And the Lord added to the church daily such as should be saved. Acts 2:46-47, KJV) What then are these wonderful works of God?

The works of God are made apparent through the misfortunes of people. If God never lets his children to through anything, then how will He demonstrate His power in our lives? God's strength is made perfect in our weakness. The Apostle Paul said, Most gladly therefore will I rather glory in my infirmities that the power of Christ may rest upon me. (11 Corinthians 12:9b, KJV). To the lame man at the gate called Beautiful: Peter said, Silver and gold have I none; but such as I have give I thee; in the name of Jesus Christ of Nazareth rise up and walk. Immediately the man's feet and ankle bones received strength. (Acts 3:2, 6, 7, KJV) Now when they saw the boldness of Peter and John, and perceived that they were unlearned and ignorant men, they marveled; and they took knowledge of them, that they had been with Jesus. (Acts 4:13, KJV) Can anyone ever detect that you have been with Jesus?

And the word of God increased; and the number of the disciples multiplied in Jerusalem greatly; and a great company of the priests were obedient to the faith. (Acts 6:7, KJV)

Peter and John had a treasure of the Lord on the inside of them. They were men full of the Holy Spirit and power. This is why they could speak the word of God with boldness. There is power in the Name of Jesus. It was so the excellency of the power was not of them, but of God.

What then are the wonderful works of God? Phillip led the Ethiopian to Christ by preaching to him Jesus and baptized him. (Acts 8:27-37, KJV) The Lord Jesus converted Saul on the Demascus road and changed his name and his life forever. He went from persecuting the church to preaching the gospel. (Acts 9, KJV) Peter was miraculously freed from prison by an angel that came to him. The church was praying for him and when she showed up at the door of the place where they were praying, they were in disbelief. (Acts 12:3,5, KJV) God does answer prayer. When we pray, we should pray with expectation, believing that God will hear and He will answer.

What then are the wonderful works of God? And at midnight Paul and Silas prayed, and sang praises unto God: and the prisoners heard them. And suddenly there was a great earthquake, so that the foundations of the prison were shaken: and immediately all the doors were opened, and everyone's bonds were loosed. (Acts 16:25,26, KJV) The keeper of the prison was afraid the prisoners had escaped. He was about to take his own life. Paul cried out in a loud voice, saying, Do thyself no harm; for we are all here. The keeper of the prison asked, what must I do to be saved? He was told to believe on the Lord Jesus Christ, and thou shalt be saved, and thy house. They spake to him the word of the Lord. He and his household were saved. (Acts 16:25-32, KJV)

What then are the wonderful works of God? When the day of Pentecost was fully come, they were all with one accord in one place. And suddenly there came a sound from heaven as of a rushing might wind, and it filled all the house where they were sitting. (Acts 2:1, KJV) The Lord poured out his Spirit as had been promised in Acts 1:8, KJV.

My brothers and sisters, we must elevate humanity, not tear them down. Stand up for the least of these. When you see humanity has fallen, raise up your brothers and sisters. Raise them up by showing them that you care. Raise them up by letting them know there is someone who cares about what they are going through and wants to help them. Encourage them in the faith by assuring them that trouble doesn't last always. Encourage them in the faith by reassuring them that weeping may endure for a night, but joy comes in the morning. (Psalm 30:5, KJV)

Encourage them in the faith by assuring them that God will fight for you if you keep still. Oh, my brothers and sisters, things might look mighty bleak sometimes, but I can guarantee you if you wait on the Lord, be of good courage, He will strengthen your heart. (Psalm 27:14, KJV)

He will come to your rescue. He may not come when you want Him, but He is always on time. He's an on time God, yes He is. He will give you beauty for ashes and the oil of joy for mourning, the garment of praise for the spirit of heaviness … (Isaiah 61:3, KJV) Do you know Him? Have you tried Him? But he was wounded for our transgressions, he was bruised for our iniquities: the chastisement of our peace was upon him; and with his stripes we are healed. (Isaiah 53:5, KJV) Healed from sins past; healed from sins present; healed from future sins. Do you know Jesus today? He is Alpha and Omega, the beginning and the end. He is the Rose of Sharon, the Lily of the Valley, the Bright and Morning Star. He is a Wonderful Counselor, the Mighty God, The Everlasting Father, Prince of Peace. He is calling to you today. "Ho, everyone that thirsteth, come ye to the waters, and he that hath no money; come ye, buy and eat; yea, come, buy wine and milk without money and without price. Wherefore do ye spend money for that which is not bread? And your labour for that which satisfieth not? Hearken(listen) diligently unto me, and eat ye that which is good, and let your soul delight itself in fatness. (Isaiah 55:1,2, KJV) God invites you to come and allow Him to quench your thirst and let him fill you with what you are hungry for. Eat from his table. He can prepare a table before you in the presence of your enemies. Stop spending your money on things that are not satisfying you. His word satisfies. Job said in Job 23:12, KJV, I desired your word more than my necessary food.

Trust wholeheartedly in the *wonderful works of God*. Jesus died on a cross for the sins of the whole world. He was buried in a borrowed tomb; but on the third day morning he arose from the dead. He conquered death, hell, and the grave. But I would not have you to be ignorant, brethren, concerning them which are asleep, that ye sorrow not even as others which have no hope. For if we believe that Jesus died and rose again, even so them also which sleep in Jesus will God bring to him. For this we say unto you by the word of the Lord, that we which are alive and remain unto the coming of the Lord shall not prevent (go before) them which are asleep. For the Lord himself shall descend from heaven with a shout, with the voice of the archangel, and with the trump of God: and the dead in Christ shall rise first: then we which are alive and remain shall be caught up together with them in the clouds, to meet the Lord in the air: and so shall we ever be with the Lord. Wherefore comfort one another with these words. (1 Thessalonians 4:13-18, KJV)

The Wonderful Work of God. As change is affected in this nation, it is not by power, nor by might but by my Spirit saith the Lord. (Zachariah 4:6b, KJV) If we are doing what we do to get the credit, then the credit we get down here is all there will be. But if we are being a change agent to give glory to God, we will be rewarded in heaven. Jesus said, Let your light so shine before men that they may see your good works and glorify your Father which is in heaven. (Matthew 5:16, KJV)

Whatever God is putting in your heart to do, do that. When you know who you are, you know who you are not to be. If we are going to effect change in this world, we must realize we are the only Bible that some people will ever read. Don't be afraid to live right in the presence of others. The Apostle Paul gives us an example in (Acts 20:19, 24, KJV), Serving the Lord with all humility of mind, and with many tears, and temptations, which befell me by lying in wait of the Jews: But none of these things move me, neither count I my life dear to myself, so that I might finish my course with joy, and the ministry, which I have received of the Lord Jesus, to testify the gospel of the grace of God. *The Wonderful Works of God.* Let us not forget that our Lord when He walked on this earth healed the sick, gave sight to the blind, cleansed the leper, bound up broken hearts, set prisoners free, preached the Good News to the poor. He has commissioned us to finish the work that he begun utilizing the power which He has given. But we have this treasure in earthen vessels that the excellency of the power may be of God and not of us. (2 Corinthians 4:7, KJV)

HOLD YOUR PEACE

But he, beckoning unto them with the hand to hold their peace, declared unto them how the Lord had brought him out of the prison. And he said, Go shew these things unto James, and to the brethren. And he departed, and went unto another place. (Acts 12:17, KJV)

Acts chapter 12 holds within it the miraculous power of God to deliver his people. The Apostle Peter had been in prison under the watchful eye of 16 soldiers, to later be given over to the people after Easter. The amazing thing, however, was that prayer was made by the church unto God for him. (Acts 12:12d, KJV) This was unceasing prayer – which means they were constantly praying about this situation. Sometimes our Father wants us to pray about certain issues until we see a breakthrough in that situation and then move on to something else. We are to have faith when we pray. The effectual fervent prayer of a righteous man availeth much. (James 5:16, KJV).

I don't know about you, but I know what prayer can do ... prayer can shut a lion's mouth; ask Daniel. Prayer can make a barren woman become fertile; ask Hannah. Our Lord says in Luke 18:1, Men ought always to pray and not faint. What a friend we have in Jesus, all our sins and griefs to bear-what a privilege to carry everything to God in prayer. Oh what peace we often forfeit- Oh, what needless pains we bear, all because we do not carry everything to God in prayer.

The Apostle Peter knew how to hold his peace even in prison; we, too, must learn to hold our peace. When Jesus had instructed the disciples to cross over to the otherside, they encountered a storm. Jesus was in the hinder part of the ship, asleep on a pillow: and they awake him, and said unto Him, Master, carest thou not that we perish? And he arose and rebuked the wind, and said unto the sea, Peace, be still, and the wind ceased and there was a great calm. When we encounter storms, trials, and misfortunes in our lives, usually the first thing we do is allow our peace to leave us because we are overwhelmed by fear and doubt and what things look like. What we fail to realize is that Jesus is with us no matter where we are, upon the land or out on a stormy sea. I believe there are least three reasons why we must learn to hold our peace in times of trouble.

First, we must hold our peace because the Lord is our peace and we should hold onto his unchanging hand. His word assures us he is our Jehovah Shalom, our Peace. Whenever we know the Lord is near, we have no need to fear because where there is faith, there is victory. When faith leaves us fear sets in and when we become fearful, we fail to think clearly and we tend to behave irrationally. I say to all, Hold you peace. Be still. The answer will come.

Many of us are not patient enough to wait and let the Lord fight for us. The Lord will trouble your enemy. An example of this is seen in the book of Exodus. The children of Israel, having left Egypt, walked through the Red Sea on dry land. The Egyptians chose to follow in hot pursuit. Notice what the word says in Exodus 14:24-26, KJV: And it came to pass, that in the morning watch the Lord looked unto the host of the Egyptians through the pillar of fire and of cloud, and troubled the host of the Egyptians.

And took off their chariot wheels, that they drave them heavily; so that the Egyptians said, Let us flee from the face of Israel; for the Lord fighteth for them against the Egyptians. And the Lord said unto Moses, stretch out thine hand over the sea, that the waters may come again upon the Egyptians, upon their chariots and upon their horsemen. When the Lord noticed that the Egyptians were catching up with his children, He troubled them. He took off their chariot wheels and made them drive heavily. Even the Egyptians recognized that there was something wrong. But it was too late. They could not move forward or backward. The Lord overthrew them in the Red Sea. Not only does God always have a plan, but His plan always work. Oftentimes we are not patient enough to wait and let the Lord fight on our behalf.

Secondly, we must hold our peace because the Lord will bring us out. No matter what you may be going through, he will bring you out. He knows; He sees; He cares what happens to you. God will bring you out. He will bring you out of darkness into his marvelous light; He will bring you out of poverty into a land of plenty. He will bring you out of a pit and set you in a palace.

Thirdly, we must hold our peace because God deals with our enemies. The face of the Lord is against them that do evil (1Peter 3:12). God speaks through Moses to the children of Israel, The Lord shall fight for you, and ye shall hold your peace. (Exodus 14:14, KJV) If people have mistreated and abused you, don't waste your time trying to get revenge. Leave them in God's hand and trust him to bring justice to your situation. Vengeance is mine. I will repay saith the Lord. It is mine to avenge, I will repay. In due time their foot will slip, their day of disaster is near and their doom rushes upon them (Deuteronomy 32:35, KJV). Job 13:5, KJV, declares, O that ye should altogether hold your peace and it shall be your wisdom. Hold your peace until you know what to do with what you know.

I challenge you to hold your peace. Put your affairs in the hand of the Master. Casting all your care upon him, for he careth for you. (1 Peter 5:7, KJV) What is peace? Peace is that calm assurance that all is well. The songwriter Horatio Spafford puts it this way: When peace like a river attends my way; when sorrows like sea billows roll. What ever my lot, Thou has taught me to say, It is well; it is well with my soul. Tho' Satan should buffet, tho trials should come, Let this blest assurance control. That Christ has regarded my helpless estate and has shed His own blood for my soul. It is well; it is well, with my soul -with my soul ... it is well; it is well ... with my soul. Hold Your Peace.

TIME WAITS FOR NO ONE

For a thousand years in thy sight are but as yesterday
when it is past, and as a watch in the night.

So teach us to number our days, that we may apply
our hearts unto wisdom. Psalm 90: 4, 12, KJV.

The Psalmist in Psalm 90 is Moses. He was well aware that God
does not view time as we view time and He is not moved by
time in the same way we are. God is not limited by time. God
is time. His word declares In the beginning God … The Lord
Jesus says of himself I am Alpha and Omega, the beginning and
the end, the first and the last. (Revelations 22:13, KJV) When
we are out of time, there is no more space for opportunities. We
are to be so careful to make good use of the time we have been
given because it does run out. Note the psalmist in verse 10 of
Psalm 90, KJV, the days of our years are threescore years and
ten; and if by reason of strength they be fourscore years, yet is
their strength labour and sorrow; for it is soon cut off, and we fly
away. God has given us a gift of time. I believe that God considers
time to be managed just as he would expect us to manage our
finances, our homes, our children or anything else over which
he has made us stewards. None of these things belong to us. We
are not owners, but stewards. Psalm 24:1, KJV states firmly, The

earth is the Lord's and the fullness thereof, the world and they that dwell therein. Time does not wait. It constantly passes. Time isn't something you can store up to use at a later date. If you don't manage your time well, someone else will be glad to fill it up with their ideas and projects for you. So to keep that from happening, you try to make use of every opportunity you have. Opportunities don't always come back around.

We must realize we can not save time or even waste time. It's going to be spent whether we use it or someone else uses it for you by putting you on their schedule. According to a statistic some time ago, we spend (8) months of our lives reading junk mail; two years of our lives playing phone tag with people who are too busy or are not answering. We spend (5) years of our lives waiting at meetings for people who are too busy to show up on time. Some of us need to learn where the off button is on the cell phone. Time is a precious gift that has been given us by God. Time waits for no one. Invest time in your family. Recognize "time stealers" in your life. Invest time in the word of God and in prayer. So when the time comes for you to realize that, hey, the joy of the Lord really is my strength, it will not be such a struggle and you can say it with confidence and conviction. It is alright to say "no." The world will continue to go on. Keep some breathing room in your life. That way when God presents you with an assignment, you won't have to say, Lord, I am too busy. Could you please ask someone else?

I can not emphasize enough, Time waits for no one. If you have not yet accepted Jesus Christ as your Lord and Saviour, now is a good time.

PRAYER

Dear heavenly Father, there is an enormous amount of evil in this world and we are running out of time. Forgive us where we have wronged a brother or a sister or You by taking matters into our own hands. Lord, help us. Give us eyes to see you in the situations we encounter; ears to hear clearly your voice, hearts to understand what your will is in the many challenges we face, courage to help bring about a change in the lives of those who desire to follow where you are leading.

Lord, save us from the routine of worry and disillusionment and help us trust that you are working all these things together for our good for those who love you and are the called according to your purpose. I thank you that you are our refuge and strength, a very present help when we are in trouble. Lord thank you for this treasure on the inside of us. We give You all the glory for it.

Help us to always be quick to hear, slow to speak and slow to wrath. (James 1:19b, KJV)

In the powerful Name of Jesus, our Savior. Amen

THE CORINTHIAN SONG

I am troubled, yet not distressed
Perplexed, but not in despair.
Cause I'm a vessel full of power, With a treasure, none can compare.

Persecuted, but not forsaken.
Cast down, but not destroyed. I'm a vessel full of power
With a treasure, from the Lord.

Source: Lyric find
Song writer: Varn McKay

About the Author

Bobbie is the proud mother of two grown sons, Thado Nakia and Dr. Terrance Nathan. She has eight adorable grandchildren: Aviance, Makayla, Thado Jeremiah, Mason, Kierstian, Kayden, Major, and Terrance, Jr. She is a minister and early retired teacher who loves Jesus and has a heart of compassion for the bereaved, broken-hearted and the oppressed.

As a child Bobbie recalls loving this man named Jesus. She later accepted Christ as her Lord and Savior after the tragic death of her brother and the suicide of her mother. She is a native of Clarksdale, Mississippi. She is a graduate of Aggie High School, and Coahoma Junior College. She is a 1972 graduate of Jackson State College; she attended two years of graduate school at the University of Mobile School of Religion. She resided for 27 years on the Mississippi Gulf Coast where she got her start in ministry and the teaching profession.

She has previously served in her local church as coordinator of Grief Care Ministry and as an organizer of Single Adult Ministry. She is a Master Grief Mentor certified by Grief Care Fellowship, Inc. Bobbie is the author of *On Eagles' Wings: Faith, Fortitude, Family* released in April 2020.

Bobbie J Hays, who has a heart for the broken in spirit, has found her greatest joy and peace in communing and spending time with God. Her messages reflect what she has discovered during private time spent in His presence. Ideas for We Have This Treasure: Messages to Encourage The Heart was birthed during a quiet time experience.